SKETCHES AND PAINTINGS

MASTERWORKS OF UKIYO-E

HOKUSAI
SKETCHES AND PAINTINGS

漫画肉筆画

by Muneshige Narazaki

adaptation by John Bester

KODANSHA INTERNATIONAL LTD.
Tokyo, New York and San Francisco

Distributors:
UNITED STATES: Kodansha International/USA Ltd., through Harper & Row, Publishers, Inc., 10 East 53rd Street, New York, New York 10022. SOUTH AMERICA: Harper & Row, International Department. CANADA: Fitzhenry & Whiteside Limited, 150 Lesmill Road, Don Mills, Ontario. MEXICO AND CENTRAL AMERICA: HARLA S. A. de C. V., Apartado 30–546, Mexico 4, D.F. BRITISH COMMONWEALTH (excluding Canada and the Far East): TABS, 7 Maiden Lane, London WC2. EUROPE: Boxerbooks Inc., Limmatstrasse 111, 8031, Zurich. AUSTRALIA AND NEW ZEALAND: Book Wise (Australia) Pty. Ltd., 104–8 Sussex Street, Sydney. THAILAND: Central Department Store Ltd., 306 Silom Road, Bangkok. HONG KONG AND SINGAPORE: Books for Asia Ltd., 30 Tat Chee Avenue, Kowloon; 65 Crescent Road, Singapore 15. THE FAR EAST: Japan Publications Trading Company, P.O. Box 5030, Tokyo International, Tokyo.

Published by Kodansha International Ltd., 2–12–21 Otowa, Bunkyo-ku, Tokyo 112 and Kodansha International/USA Ltd., 10 East 53rd Street, New York, New York 10022 and 44 Montgomery Street, San Francisco, California 94104.

LCC 69–16371
ISBN 0–87011–076–4
JBC 0371–780775–2361

First edition, 1969
Third printing, 1976

Contents

ACKNOWLEDGEMENTS

For permission to reproduce paintings, prints and sketches from their collections the publishers wish to thank the following institutions and people: Mr. Eisaku Oda, Pl.1; Mr. Shōichirō Nakajima, Pls.2–3; Mr. Takeo Ujiie, Pl.4; Atami Art Museum, Pls. 5–6; Mr. Jōji Kanzaki, Pls.7–8; Shin Kenkō Kyōkai, Pl.9; Mr. Tetsuji Yura, Pl.10; British Museum, Pl.11; Mr. Hinosuke Hirose, Pls.12–14; Freer Gallery, Pls.75–79; sketches courtesy of Mr. Jūzō Suzuki and Mr. Chūsuke Tsuiji.

Hokusai and His Art

HOKUSAI IS said to have been born in the ninth month of the year 1760, the son of a man named Kawamura. He was born in the Honjo district, a low-lying marshy area where the poor of the great city of Edo eked out their humble lives. The district lay in Katsushika county of the province of Shimofusa; thus Hokusai took "Katsushika" as his surname, and even late in life would sometimes refer to himself as "the peasant from Katsushika." His fondness for using many different artistic pseudonyms was notorious even in an age when it was common for a man with artistic or literary pretensions to use several for various purposes, but it is as Katsushika Hokusai that he is most commonly known today.

Nothing is known of his father or of any of his brothers or sisters, but it seems that at the age of four or five he was adopted by a man named Nakajima Ise, a mirror-maker to the Tokugawa shogunate. Although he left this adopted home while still a boy, he made occasional use of the name Nakajima ever after.

The reason for leaving his adopted home may well have been a disinclination to spend his life polishing mirrors. In fact, from what both Hokusai and others wrote, it seems that he showed an extraordinary interest in pictures from his early childhood. In a note to his "Hundred Views of Mt. Fuji," published in his later life, he recalls that by the age of six he was already fond of drawing things for himself, and other sources date the start of his artistic career from the age of five or seven.

According to one tradition Hokusai went to work for a lending library when he left the Nakajima home. The story, though unverifiable, has the ring of truth. In an age when the masses had to rely on the small "temple schools" (*tera-koya*) run by the priests for their education, publishing houses and libraries were the ideal school for a poor youth with intellectual curiosity.

In such an environment, the young Hokusai would have had ample opportunity to see the novelettes and tales of martial prowess popular at the time. Should his taste have run to the more sophisticated variety of publication, there were picture books and illustrated tales by Hishikawa Moronobu, Torii Kiyonaga and Okumura Masanobu, and by the Kyoto artist Nishikawa Sukenobu. Moreover, Hokusai was subjected to the added stimulus of a revolution in the world of prints that occurred when he was only five. Until that time, both illustrated books and single-sheet prints had been done only in black monochrome or in the very restricted number of colors of the *tan-e* and *beni-e*. But in 1765 Suzuki Harunobu produced the first true polychrome print, paving the way for the work of such men as Kiyonaga, Utamaro and Sharaku, and for Hokusai himself.

It is not known how long Hokusai was apprenticed to the lending library—assuming the tradition to be true—but one record says that around the age of fifteen or sixteen he went to study under a woodblock engraver with the aim of following the same trade himself. Various methods of printing were known at the time. After much study a technique of etching was developed in 1783 by the artist-scientist Shiba Kōkan; the lithograph was not unknown, and in the Kyoto-Osaka area a kind of stencil was occasionally used. Nevertheless, the wooden block was overwhelmingly popular compared with other media because it offered both higher artistic potential and facilitation of mass production. An ukiyo-e print was the joint product of three craftsmen: the designer of the original, the engraver and the printer. The skill of all three was of course essential to its success, yet however admirable the original design, the whole enterprise ultimately depended on the engraver, whose duty it was to ensure that the individual flavor of the original and the artist's skill in using line were adequately conveyed in the finished work.

It is not difficult to imagine that the young Hokusai would have been attracted to the craft, seeing the splendid results achieved by engravers with the work of Harunobu, Shunshō and Kiyomitsu. But it is no more difficult to imagine that a man of his extraordinary, restless talent and strong individuality would have been unable to endure the subjection of the self and the more or less routine repetition of uninteresting chores that apprenticeship in such a trade required. Moreover, although it was the custom during the first two or three years of the polychrome print to inscribe the name of the printer and engraver alongside that of the artist, this practice was soon abandoned and both dropped back into the anonymous obscurity of the craftsman. Whatever his motive, however, Hokusai must in fact have laid aside his chisel by the time he was eighteen, for at that age he became a pupil of Katsukawa Shunshō, one of the most celebrated ukiyo-e artists of the day.

Something should be said here of the culture in which Hokusai grew up, for it was this culture that, despite his differences from his contemporaries, determined in great measure the nature of his art. Perhaps the most striking feature of the arts of the day, with the exception of the devitalized art of the "official" schools, was the faithfulness with which they reflected the spirit of the "merchant" class—which meant, in practice, not only the merchants, but the small shopkeepers, the artisans, the low-ranking samurai—in short, the great mass of the common people as distinct from the "establishment" of the time. This spirit is equally detectable in the haiku of Buson, in the ukiyo-e, in the humorous verse such as the *senryū* (17-syllable) and *kyōka* (31-syllable), in the kabuki drama, in the popular music with samisen accompaniment and in the popular literature, where a new type of novelette known as *kibyōshi* ("yellow cover") was just coming into its own. Its characteristics include a great sensitivity to the change of the seasons and to the ritual details of everyday life, in which a maximum of enjoyment was found, an indifference to problems outside the daily lives of the people for whom the art was intended; a wit and sophistication that were urbane, wry and involuted to an almost unhealthy degree; and a gayness and frivolity that partly counterbalanced the heavy weight of official Confucianist morality.

Two centuries after the founding of the Tokugawa shogunate, which had established its seat of government in Edo, the focal point of merchant culture had finally shifted from the Osaka-Kyoto area to what was now the huge, thriving capital. Its home lay not in the higher, more salubrious districts around the shogun's castle where the feudal lords and higher-ranking samurai had their mansions, but on the flatland flanking the Sumida River and its tributaries. Here the common people lived and flourished within their own complex yet peculiarly confined world. Prosperous yet condemned under a feudal regime to the lowest position of all within a hierarchical society, the merchants found insufficient normal outlets for their energies and their wealth, so they devoted themselves instead to the details of their own lives, and to amusements such as the theater and the gay quarters. The results were the observance of a multitude of small rituals that gave variety and interest to daily life, and the establishment of all kinds of entertainment facilities. Yet the fact remained that in everything important the claims of society came before those of the individual—even before those of family. This led to a sense of futility that brought in turn a sense of resignation, and out of this developed the characteristic light-heartedness of much Edo art. The Edo merchant replaced the Osaka merchant's sterner outlook and preoccupation with the acquisition of wealth by a more frivolous, spendthrift attitude. And in the gay quarters of the Yoshiwara he created a carefree world that had its own rules yet permitted a kind of self-expression and human contact that life under the Tokugawa regime did not otherwise contain.

It was this world that provided the subject matter for a large proportion of ukiyo-e. What they did not normally show was the enormous cost in human suffering, especially among the women who were the center of that world, or the poverty and hardship in the provinces, which felt the full effects of the failure of the shogunate's economic policies, and from which many of these women had, in desperation, first come. It is one of Hokusai's characteristics that he spanned both worlds, for his work covered not only the conventional beauty of the ukiyo-e, but the peasants toiling in the fields (notably in the *Sketches* and the "Thirty-six Views of Mt. Fuji"), with, in between, a wide range of ordinary townsfolk from almost every possible walk of life (the *Sketches*). He added to the achievements of the ukiyo-e an earthy realism and humor and an underlying compassion that were comparatively rare in other artists.

In the contemporary world of art and ideas, there was a great deal to stimulate the young Hokusai. Harunobu, whose work marked a great stride forward for the ukiyo-e print, was only the greatest of the many artists, such as Ippitsusai Bunchō and Isoda Koryūsai, who worked in much the same style. In Hokusai's youth, the Okumura school, which had reached its peak in the Genroku (1688–1704) and Kyōhō (1716–1736) eras was still lingering on, while the artists of the Kaigetsudō school, as well as Ishikawa Toyonobu, were still working—though by the Hōreki era (1751–1754) most of them had faded into obscurity. The famous Torii school seemed in danger of dying out, but one of its pupils, Kiyonaga, was soon to become its fourth head; the school was to revive, and Kiyonaga himself was to become the leading figure in the field of *bijin-ga* (pictures of beautiful women) during the Temmei era (1781–1789). The line that had begun with Miyagawa Chōshun ran, via Shunsui to Katsukawa Shunshō, one of the idols of the Temmei and Kansei (1789–1801) eras who formed a school of his own and with whom Hokusai himself was to study.

All these artists brought new life to existing family lines. Besides these, however, the golden age of the Temmei and Kansei eras included new groups such as the Kitao school (Shigemasa and his pupils Masanobu and Masayoshi), the Toriyama school (Toriyama Sekien and his pupils Utamaro, Harumatsu and Chōki), the Utagawa school (the founder Toyoharu and his pupils Toyokuni and Toyohiro), the Eishi school (Chōbunsai Eishi and pupils such as Eishō and Eiri); and the great Sharaku, who so far as we know today stood all alone, a solitary peak among the other great ranges. In the Kyoto-Osaka area, the genre picture was kept in energetic life by Nishikawa Sukenobu's artistic progeny, by Tsukioka Settei and his school in Kyoto and by various artists in Osaka, while the artists of the Maruyama Shijō school founded by Maruyama Ōkyo vied with the artists of Edo by painting the manners and customs of their own city, Kyoto.

In the field of painting, this was the period of some of the great artists of the Japanese "Literati" school—men such as Ike-no-Taiga, or in a slightly different vein, the haiku poet Buson, who produced works that were a blend of picture and poetry. Other masters were Goshun in Kyoto and Tani Bunchō in Edo.

Farther south, in Nagasaki, there was a new burst of interest in Western learning as brought to Japan by the Dutch. It was in 1572 that Hiraga Gennai visited Nagasaki, and in 1757 Sugita Gempaku made his celebrated exposition of Western surgery. Around the same time, Ōkyo was experimenting with new effects in Western perspective, and in 1774 Odano Naotake transcribed the Dutch textbook of anatomy known in Japanese as *Kaitai Shinsho*. It was in 1783 that Shiba Kōkan, already mentioned above, first discovered how to make etchings.

Thus there were new ideas and new techniques in the air, despite the stagnation of society as a whole. Even in the political sphere, there were the first signs of the great upheavals that were due in the not so distant future. In 1767, a plot to overthrow the shogunate came to light. The principals were executed, but the incident served to cast doubt on the stability of what had seemed an unshakable regime. In a sense, all the activity in the world of art that we have just outlined above could be seen as a bursting out of pent-up energies, a series of gestures against the rigid formalism of the schools such as the Kanō and Tosa that represented the official taste in art.

It was at such a time, then, that Hokusai, still a young man, became a pupil of the great Katsukawa Shunshō, and traces of the time through which he lived are to be found, not only in the subject matter and spirit of his work, but also in the varying techniques that he used at different times. Yet, as is often the case with a great and long-lived genius, he was late in maturing. In his twenties and thirties he tried his hand at many things, without achieving any conspicuous success. His polychrome prints at this time were mostly put out by second-rate publishers. Though he did actor-pictures, *bijin-ga*, and scenes from Edo life, they were poorly printed, and the An'ei, Temmei, and Kansei eras (1772–1801)—those great years in the history of the ukiyo-e—slipped by without his having produced any true masterpiece. Moreover, although he had become the pupil of a famous artist, he seems from the start to have had trouble in fitting into patterns and conforming.

Shunshō, Hokusai's teacher, had achieved his fame with his portraits of actors, which broke out of the formalism into which the actor-pictures of the Torii school had lapsed. He also did pictures of sumo wrestlers and warriors, but he seems to have been content to leave prints of beautiful women to men such as Kiyonaga and Utamaro. From his middle years on, he seems gradually to have withdrawn from the world of prints and devoted himself increasingly to painting pictures of women, probably for some wealthy patron. Many of his pupils followed suit. Hokusai, however, showed little interest in painting at this stage—but he did not produce anything outstanding in the way of actor-pictures, either.

This was the situation when Shunshō died. Hokusai himself was already thirty-three at the time. Following the master's death, the school gradually disintegrated. Hokusai himself studied with a succession of other masters, beginning with one Yūsen of the Kanō school. This "dilettantism" was no doubt one of the factors, combined with his uncompromising personality, that accounted for his expulsion from the Katsukawa school in 1794, three years after Shunshō's death.

In 1795, Hokusai assumed the name Tawaraya Sōri II. The first Sōri had been a pupil of Sumiyoshi Hiromori of the Sumiyoshi school of *Yamato-e*. Around this time he was expelled from the Kanō school, some say because of a personal difference with Yūsen. His quest for a style also took him to study with another painter, Tsutsumi Tōrin, and to dabble in both Chinese and Western styles of painting. His first use of the pseudonym Hokusai dates from this period.

The next year, Hokusai was forty. At last after many years of artistic wandering and shifting allegiances, he found himself on his own, and it is from now that he began to display his full creative powers. This does not mean, of course, that his years as Sōri II had been wasted, for his activities during that time had extended over a very great range, including single-sheet prints, picture books and book illustrations, paintings, pictures of beautiful women, actor-pictures and landscapes. It was as though he was preparing for what was to come, testing out the relationship that his art was to form with nature and with humanity.

Hokusai's achievement between the age of forty and his death was so varied and so great in quantity that no detailed consideration of it is possible in a short space. His vitality—the vitality that made him talk at the age of seventy-five of what his art would have achieved by the time he was 110—can be better appreciated when one remembers that in Hokusai's day forty was considered to be the beginning of old age, and fifty to be a reasonable life-span.

These years from 1799 to 1849 were a period of change and restlessness in the world at large. By the beginning of the period, the great artists who had carried the ukiyo-e through its golden age were either dead or declining and new men were rising to take their place. The first twenty years or so of the nineteenth century were noted for a new type of brilliance in the arts: overripe—decadent, perhaps—yet without the meretricious element that affected so much of the work produced at the very end of the Edo period. There was a general air of restlessness and change. The shogunate's policies both economic and political were reaching an impasse. There was talk of restoring the emperor to his rightful position, of the claims of loyalty, of treason. The feudal system that had gripped the country tight for so long was loosening its hold; the dissemination of printed matter, both prints and books, was making the nation one as it had never been before. It was becoming genuinely possible to talk of a nationwide popular culture. Although the culture of the merchant class of Edo in this period was indeed decadent in one sense, it was also in another sense an upsurging of the need for self-expression of the lower classes of society. In Edo the popular arts and entertainments flourished as never before. Throughout the nation as a whole there was a new interest in travel and in visiting famous scenic spots. The reading public swelled enormously. These last two facts were to account in part for the hold that Hokusai maintained over the public during the years of his maturity.

The greatest organized force in the world of ukiyo-e in this period was the Utagawa school. Toyohiro was succeeded by Hiroshige, and Toyokuni's pupils included Kunisada and Kuniyoshi and dozens of others who turned out vast quantities of kabuki pictures and pictures of voluptuous women. Two other artists, Kikugawa Eizan and Kikugawa Eisen, worked in much the same vein. The aesthetic concept that presided over all their art was that of *iki*—a purely Edo concept of chic containing elements of the sophisticated, the stylish, and the refined, with a dash of sex thrown in, the whole realized in terms of the highly organized, suppressed, inward-turned and in a sense, unhealthy society of the day.

Hokusai stood somewhat apart from this activity. He could not ignore it, of course, and he produced actor-pictures and *bijin-ga* like the rest. But he was not and never could have been a dyed-in-the-wool Edoite like Kunisada or Eisen with the special type of sophistication—and the special type of limitations—that that implied. By the opening years of the nineteenth century he was a prominent figure in the world of art, with dozens of pupils his own, but it was still chiefly as illustrators that they were active. In this field Hokusai inaugurated a new style of his own, noted for its surpassing precision and power, skillful composition and lifelike human figures. In particular, his illustrations for the fanciful and grotesque tales of the author Kyokutei Bakin won him great fame throughout the capital.

Another great achievement of this first period, (roughly the years from the age of forty to the age of fifty), lay in the field of *kyōka ehon*. These were a kind of *meisho zue*, black and white illustrated guides to scenic spots throughout the country. There was great vogue for these and they did much to enhance the general public's awareness of the land in which they lived, but Hokusai's works, the *kyōka ehon*, were done in very elaborate color and would have been available only to the wealthier classes. In works such as *Azuma Asobi, Sumidagawa Ryōgan Ichiran*, and *Yama Mata Yama*, he portrayed the capital's famous sights and its inhabitants with a romantic, poetic touch. Various sets of scenes on the Tōkaidō highway provided a kind of visual counterpart to the picturesque and picaresque literature of Jippensha Ikku.

A third and perhaps most striking achievement of this period was his experiments with landscape pictures making use of the techniques of Western painting. In some works, such as the *Edo Hakkei* and *Ōmi Hakkei,* he made use of blocks cut across the grain as in Western prints or used a woodblock style heavily influenced by the etching. In others, such as *Kudan Ushigafuchi, Yotsuya Jūniso* and *Takahashi,* he applied Western-style perspective, chiaroscuro and shading in an astonishingly modern manner; here he does not merely record nature objectively, but treats it as material for creating forms of subjective significance.

For some years Hokusai continued to produce illustrations for popular tales in the new manner that he had originated, but it seems that the general tendency to look on the illustrations in such works as secondary in importance, designed merely to make the books interesting to the "inferior" minds of women and children, irked him somewhat, and towards his mid-fifties he gradually decreased his output. Instead, he gradually increased the number of polychrome prints he produced. Then in his later fifties he began to turn out an increasing number of manuals on painting and sketching. Thus the *Ryakuga Haya-shinan* (1812) was followed by *Hokusai Shashin Gafu* (1814), *Santai Gafu* (1815) and *Ehon Hayabiki* (1817). Although these are referred to as "manuals," they were also intended, of course, to give pleasure. This is particularly evident in his celebrated series of *Sketchbooks*, which began in 1814 and ended, in theory, with vol. 10 in 1819, though in fact they continued even after that date. The extraordinary manner in which he brought to life all manner of men, all manner of natural phenomena, with a maximum economy of line made his *Sketchbooks* the rage of all Japan and astonished the West when he was discovered there. Moreover, the influence that these works and others of their kind had in educating the public in a country where art had tended to be something of a closed shop should not be overlooked.

During his sixties Hokusai continued various kinds of artistic activities, but he does not seem to have made any great strides forward. It was formerly believed that his masterpiece, the "Thirty-six Views of Mt. Fuji," was begun during this period, around 1823, but in fact it was probably later than this; what is certain is that its publication was still in progress in 1831, when Hokusai was seventy-one. This work, a set of forty-six prints (including ten added to the original series), marked the peak of his achievement as a landscape artist in the inventiveness of the composition, the use of color, the sense of atmosphere and the faithful rendition of the natural and human scene. His triumph was overshadowed, however, by the publication of Hiroshige's *Tōto Meisho* (Kawaguchi version), which with other works of the same period marked a definite swing in the public favor away from Hokusai and towards Hiroshige.

Hokusai followed up the "Thirty-six Views" with a whole series of fine works, including *Chie no Umi*, *Shokoku Taki-mawari*, *Ryūkyū Hakkei*, and *Shokoku Meikyō Kiran*, as well as a number of prints on "flower-and-bird" themes. Nevertheless, they could not rival the growing popular appeal of Hiroshige's landscapes and flower-and-bird pictures. It seems that Hokusai's refusal to compromise with popular taste and his intensely personal style had begun to cloy with the general public.

The competition intensified. Hiroshige was soon at the height of his creativity, and other artists such as Eisen, Kunisada and Kuniyoshi also published landscapes with considerable success. In 1834, at the age of seventy-four, Hokusai published "One Hundred Views of Mt. Fuji," a series of prints in book form using various shades of black Chinese ink without color. It was a notable achievement in terms of both printing techniques and artistic content, but it was to be his last major work. The fifteen years between then and his death mark an undeniable decline, and he was no longer in the front rank of the ukiyo-e world. He frequently did illustrations, but now the subjects were usually imaginary and historical, inspired by themes such as the Confucian virtues, Chinese poetry, tales of famous battles, the life of Buddha, and so on. He also produced some single-sheet prints on genre subjects, but in this sphere he had definitely lost the power to interest the public.

Like many ukiyo-e artists, he seems to have found solace in his old age in painting, and quite a few of his finest works of this type date from his last years.

He died on the eighteenth day of the fourth month of 1849 at the age of ninety. His ashes were interred at the Seikyōji temple at Nagazumi-chō in the Asakusa district, where his grave still stands to this day.

The great haiku poet Bashō stressed the need for the artist, having perceived the higher truth, to return to the everyday world. Another haiku master, Buson, believed that the means of release from the world should be ordinary, everyday words. Both, knowing that actuality is not necessarily elegant—that it is more often vulgar or even ugly—were criticizing the concept of art as an elegant pursuit remote from actuality, and in the view of the artist of the Edo period there was indeed an unmistakable element of escapism, of seeking to prettify the real world.

From the outset, Hokusai was no escapist; he was of the earth, of the world, and he had a restless dynamism that somehow seemed to identify itself with the nature that he saw at work about him. Hokusai surveyed this fluctuating variety of phenomena—the great and the small, the admirable and the ridiculous alike—and projected them into his art as if they were an extension of his own person. In many of Hokusai's works, there is no single focus of interest; the focal point is the whole picture itself, within which details are supplied painstakingly and with the clarity of something seen in broad daylight.

The human beings and society that appear in his works are all subjected to an almost cruelly insistent will. They form, as it were, mandalas in which the central deity is really the self, Hokusai's self. It is somehow appropriate that Hokusai should have been an adherent of the Nichiren sect, which is noted among the sects of Japanese Buddhism for its activism, its egoism and its exclusivism. Such a person as Hokusai, always living in the present, can never achieve enlightenment in any conventional sense; he is forever discontented, incomplete, at variance with others and isolated.

In Hokusai, there was a touch of solitary arrogance. In his long life of ninety years he saw society change, his pupils desert him and even his own family go their separate ways. His blind self-assurance and sense of the superiority of his own art were responsible for a private life that was unconventional, to say the least. His belief in art as his sole mission and his fierce devotion to himself as an artist made him seem, in the eyes of his contemporaries, the very incarnation of willfulness—a cold, stubborn, difficult eccentric. It is no wonder that his disciples dropped away one by one: the way of the artist as he conceived it was not to be imitated easily.

Fame and wealth as such did not concern him. Although at the height of his fame he was revered as the "sage of painting" in what was in effect the nation's capital, and was surrounded by all the temptations of the gay life, he never became a typical man-about-town or dilettante, but retained something unpolished and earthy. Like the peasant, he was free only so long as he was working and producing.

He was the first Japanese artist to discern that actuality could, in itself, be a subject for art. In this one senses something basically different from his fellow artists. Most Japanese artists have agreed with the sages and saints of old in looking beyond the restlessness, the imperfection and the ugliness of the world to something still and abiding. Sesshū and Bashō were alike in seeking the still center that lay at the heart of things.

Hokusai, it seems, was an exception to this rule. For him, it was precisely in the incomplete and differentiated that the truth lay. Their restless movement was, in itself, the essence of the universe. And it was this that he depicted in his art. His human figures are shown going about their business or their pleasure—but never depicted simply standing. Birds and beasts, even his landscapes are all in motion. The celebrated "Great Wave off Kanagawa" in the "Thirty-six Views"—that dramatic arresting of the sea in violent motion—is only the most famous example of this. Everything right down to rocks, water, clouds and mountains is felt in Hokusai's work as a momentary aspect of the life of the universe, and as such seems to be straining to launch into motion. Even the "Red Fuji" (with the "Great Wave," one of the two most famous works in the "Thirty-six Views"), so static at first glance, in fact represents one particular moment on one particular day when the sun, piercing the pre-dawn darkness, first brought a flush to the mountain's flanks. The next moment, everything would be different again.

The advocate of passive enlightenment might object to this attitude and ascribe it to a naive over-confidence in the self. Man cannot, in fact, know even himself, much less the universe, completely. To see all creation as "life" or as "energy" is no more—it might be claimed—than to project oneself onto the universe. And it is true that in this sense Hokusai was the supreme subjectivist. In his work we witness a succession of subjective experiences—the repetition and continuation of such experiences was the only type of eternity he could know.

All the things that Hokusai depicts, his people, his society, his plants, his fish, are in a sense projections of the artist, charged with his own will and destiny. Looking through Hokusai's sketches, one begins to be aware, not so much of the astonishing sureness with which so many varying phenomena are captured, as of the sardonic, ever-shifting personality of Hokusai himself. Here is the stage of life, with Hokusai as the director. Japanese art had never before produced such a vital, far-ranging and essentially "unrefined" master.

MUNESHIGE NARAZAKI

1. *The Assignation Boat* ◆ 9.4 × 11.8 inches (23.9 × 30.0 cm.). ◆ painting on silk ◆ The woman shown here is one of the low-grade prostitutes who plied their trade from boats moored off the wharves that lined the Sumida River in old Edo. Her face has a remote, classical quality that would hardly be out of place on a Bodhisattva in earlier art, but the black hood blowing in the chill river breeze and the footwarmer against which she huddles clearly depict the wretched lot of such women. The work is one of a set of twelve paintings done in collaboration with Toyokuni and others. It dates from the artist's fifties, probably the latter half.

2. *Gathering Shellfish at Low Tide* ◆ 21.3 × 33.8 inches (54.5 × 86.6 cm.) ◆ painting on silk ◆ One of Hokusai's most famous paintings dating from the early Bunka era, when he was in his late forties, this work succeeds remarkably in capturing what must have been a typical scene on the seashore not far from Edo. Especially skillful is the treatment of space: in the foreground are the large figures of the women and the fisherman, balanced on the left by the three children playing happily in the breakers; in the middle distance is a line of small figures such as often occurs in Hokusai's landscape prints, together with a group of fishing vessels; and in the background is a line of distant mountains beneath a sky treated in a manner reminiscent of oil painting, with the white cone of Mt. Fuji visible in the still remoter distance on the left.

3. Detail from painting on opposite page.

4. *Beauty in Her Cups* ◆ 10.3 × 12.7 inches (26.5 × 32.5 cm.) ◆ painting on silk ◆ This work, though physically small, is one of the finest of all Hokusai's *bijin-ga*. It dates from around 1808, a time when Hokusai, now at his creative best, was devoting much of his energy to illustrative work with painting as an important sideline. The woman portrayed here is slightly tipsy and supports herself against a lacquered chest, her head resting pensively on her hand. Her erotic appeal with a suggestion of helplessness shows that, for all his individualism, Hokusai could still produce work in the true tradition of the ukiyo-e.

5. Detail from painting on opposite page.

6. *Two Beautiful Women* ◆ 43.1 × 14.3 inches (110.5 × 36.7 cm.) ◆ painting on silk ◆ Hokusai made this painting in his forties, probably the early years, and it shows that even after relinquishing the title of Sōri II he still had occasion to do works with a strongly romantic flavor. The two women shown here, voluptuous yet fresh and youthful, mark a kind of transitional stage between the frail, stooping figures of his early period and the older, more robust women that he preferred from his fifties onward.

7–8. *Spring and Autumn* ◆ painting on silk ◆ A graceful, brilliantly colored pair of figures in the full tradition of the ukiyo-e *bijin-ga*. "Autumn," on the left, watches fireflies glowing in a small cage she holds in her hands, and "Spring," on the right, delicately holds out her fan before a background of hills covered with cherry trees in bloom. The works were painted when Hokusai was fifty-three and represent a transitional phase between his middle and late periods.

9. *The Tanabata Festival* ◆ 37.4 × 10.5 inches (96 × 28.1 cm.) ◆ painting on paper ◆ The Tanabata Festival on the seventh day of the seventh month marked the day when it was believed that the Herdsboy and the Weaver, two heavenly lovers separated from each other throughout the rest of the year by the Milky Way, were reunited for a single night of love. It was a popular belief in Japan that young maidens of the type portrayed here would have their dearest wish granted on this day. The work dates from Hokusai's middle years; the women in his later pictures have lost the fresh, delicate charm of this figure.

10. *The Monkey Trainer* ◆ 11.9×23.6 inches (28.0×60.0 cm.) ◆ painting on paper ◆ One of the finer works of Hokusai's old age, this painting is part of a series showing characteristic sights of the city from each month of the year. The economy and sensitivity of the brushwork is particularly remarkable, and skillful use is made of the delicate coloring in order to suggest movement.

曲亭馬琴題

11. *Tametomo Routing the Demons With His Bow* ◆ painting on paper ◆ British Museum, London ◆ This work is a product of the celebrated collaboration between Hokusai and the novelist Kyokutei Bakin, who was famed for his bizarre and fanciful tales. During the years from 1806–1810 Hokusai illustrated successive volumes of a "historical" work by Bakin centering around the exploits of Minamoto Tametomo and his wondrous bow, then in 1811, when Hokusai was 51, he did this painting for which Bakin himself wrote the commentary inscribed in the upper left-hand corner. Hokusai here proves to be an admirable match for Bakin's power and imagination. The violent motion of the figures is skillfully echoed in the pine trees straining in the wind and in the waves that dash against the nearby shore.

12–14. *Scene Eleven from Chūshingura* ◆ three *ōban* color prints ◆ Hokusai produced this work during the period when he was still a pupil of Katsukawa Shunshō, although he already had many pupils of his own at the time. *Chūshingura* is the famous tale—especially celebrated in its kabuki form—of the revenge and subsequent suicide of the "Forty-seven Loyal Retainers." This scene is the bloody assault by night on the mansion of their hated enemy, Lord Kira. The work is crowded but there is mastery in the detail and in the colors set against the black backdrop of the night sky, and the whole picture has the sense of restless movement characteristic of Hokusai.

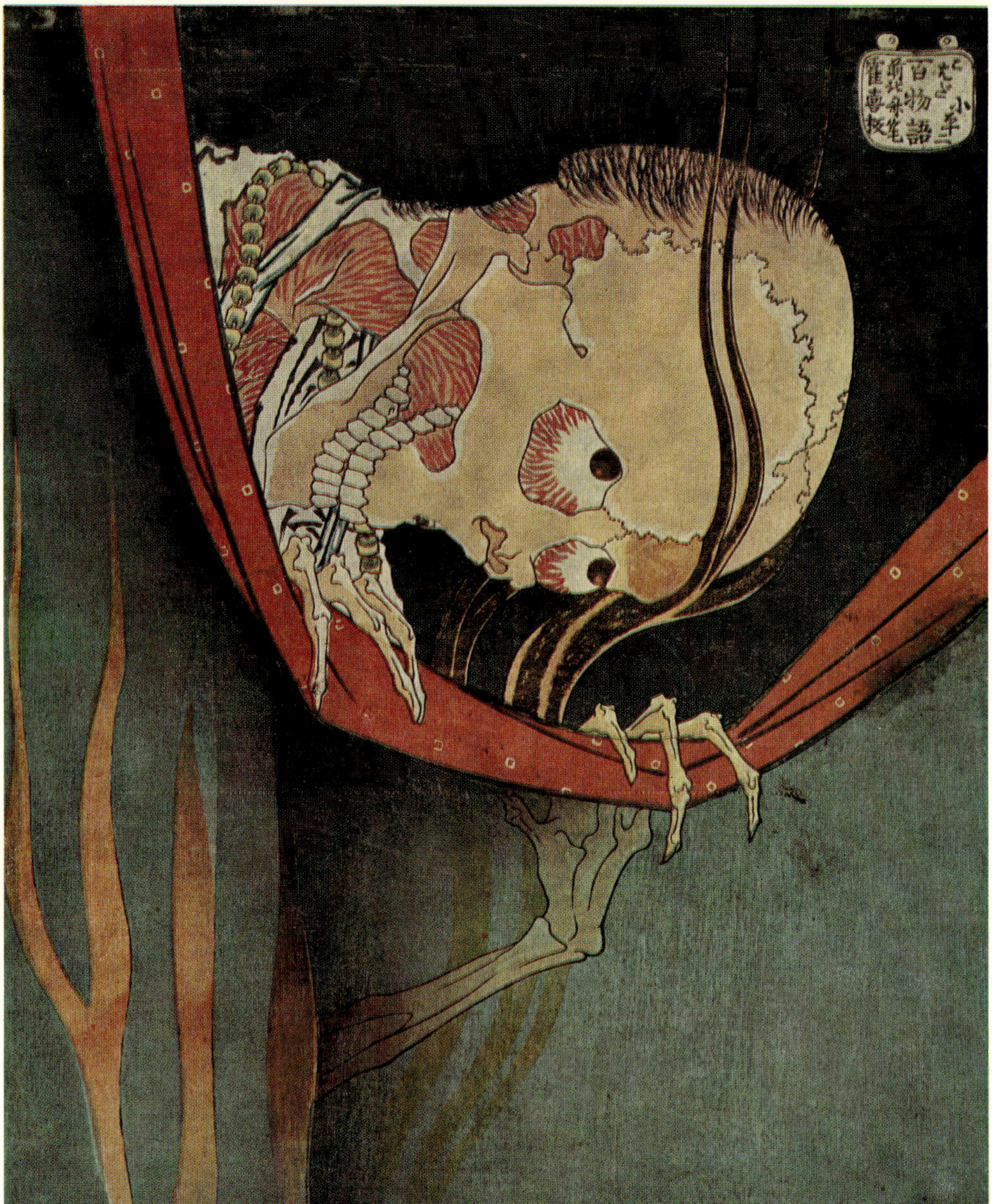

15. *Kohada Koheiji from "One Hundred Tales"* ◆ *chūban* color print ◆ published by Tsuruki ◆ Five other works based on macabre tales of the kind popular in the Edo period are known today, but it is not clear how many prints the series originally comprised. Pictures of this kind were popular in Hokusai's day, but artistically this is one of the most successful of all. Copies of the original edition are very rare; most of those extant come from a new edition made in the Meiji era.

16. A miscellany of animal and human figures in which Hokusai seems to be showing how to grasp the essentials of a form or posture using a minimum number of brushstrokes. The human figures are especially skillfully done: the wandering monk playing his flute at the top right-hand corner; the woman beckoning someone (in Japanese fashion, with palm held downwards) next to him; the old man with a mortar and pestle; the man making a tub (who appears again in one of Hokusai's "Thirty-six Views of Mt. Fuji"); the courtesan in all her finery at the bottom left, contrasting so strongly with the housewife next to her, who might well be on her way to go shopping; and the old man swatting a mosquito with his fan in the bottom right-hand corner. As often in ukiyo-e, the dog is surprisingly unconvincing.

17-18. On these two pages, Hokusai deals with groups of people. The lower half of the left-hand page shows a scene in a public bathhouse. The doorkeeper on his raised dais, cashbox by his side, is engrossed in his book, seemingly indifferent to the women in front of him. Note the women undressing at the upper right of the group, the child playing with water and the woman with the cloth tied around her waist, a sign that she is pregnant. The upper group shows a noodle vendor and a man returning home with his bundle on his back, the lantern between them indicating that it is night; a woman with her apron still on and a child on her back—the classic pose of the wife who has finished preparing the evening meal and is wait-

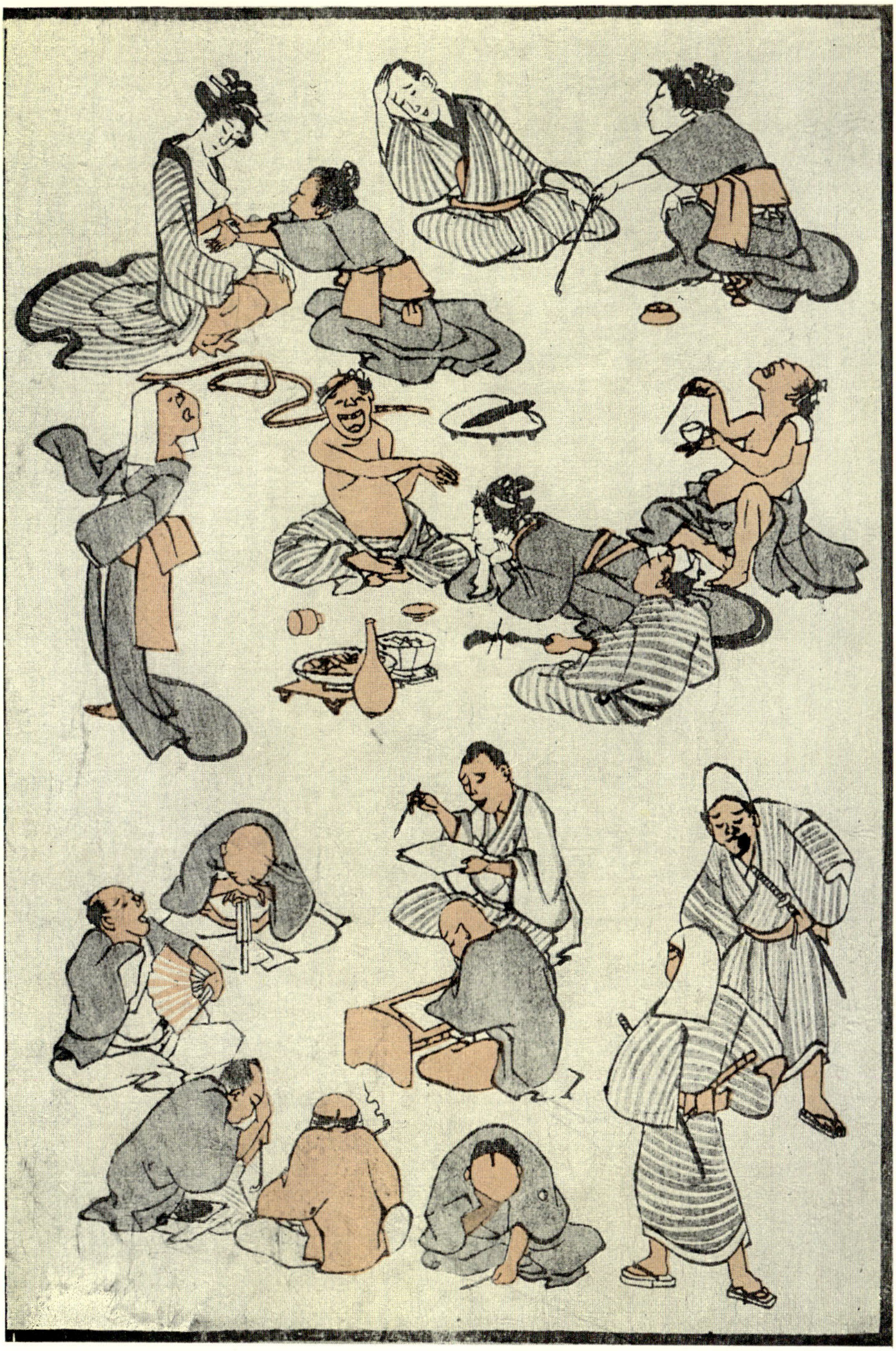

ing for her husband to return home; a maidservant with a lantern lighting the way for someone, probably a high-ranking courtesan; and a man at home relaxing over a cup of tea before beginning his evening meal.

The upper half of the right-hand page shows a woman being examined by the midwife; a wife scolding her husband, who looks embarrassed (probably at having been detected in some unfaithfulness); and a drinking party where things have just got to the stage at which people have the urge to get up and dance. The lower half shows, on the left, a haiku-composing party, wonderfully capturing the postures of the man reciting and his friends, who either listen intently or are themselves composing.

19. At the top right, two men are shown making *dengaku* (a kind of glutinous cake made from devil's-tongue root, toasted on sticks and dipped in fermented soybean paste), while in the foreground a party of men and women are far gone in a drinking party. One can only marvel at the skill with which Hokusai, despite his enormous output, could give instant and identifiable reality to each posture and gesture of his characters.

20. A group of men and women are searching for *matsutake*, a type of edible mushroom highly prized in Japan. The two women have been lucky, and are looking pleased with themselves. The man in the lower right-hand corner has also found one, which he is holding aloft while his companion rejoices. It is not clear what the other two men are gesturing so excitedly about—possibly they are summoning other companions not shown in the picture.

21-22. *Fat People*. The title to these two pages means something like "Hokusai-Style Humorous Pictures," and the sixteen men and women shown are all fat in a way liable to provoke a good-natured smile. The woman taking a nap with her kimono pushed back off her shoulders; the man nodding over some long epistle; the pot-bellied man at lower right for whom the act of scratching his back seems such an effort—all of them, even the cat, have a rounded, com-

fortable air. On the right-hand page, the handling of the expressions of the three men whose faces are visible is a marvel of economy, and the gait of the three fat women shown walking is captured admirably.

23-24. Enlarged details from Plates 21-22. It is a tribute to Hokusai's mastery that his small sketches, such as these, should stand up to enlargement and actually benefit from it.

the right-hand page shows a drinking party at which all the men and women are fat, while below them are a fat man looking languidly up at the sky, a man sitting down to rest and wipe off the sweat, and a fat woman squatting in a tub.

27–28. *Abundant Harvest*. The two pages are divided horizontally, the upper half showing a stretch of farmland in late autumn, after the rice has been harvested, with nothing left but the birds wheeling about in search of fallen ears. The lower section shows peasants making merry. Nowadays, with the great advances made in cultivation techniques, a poor harvest is something unheard of, but in the Edo period damage from flood, drought, and frost

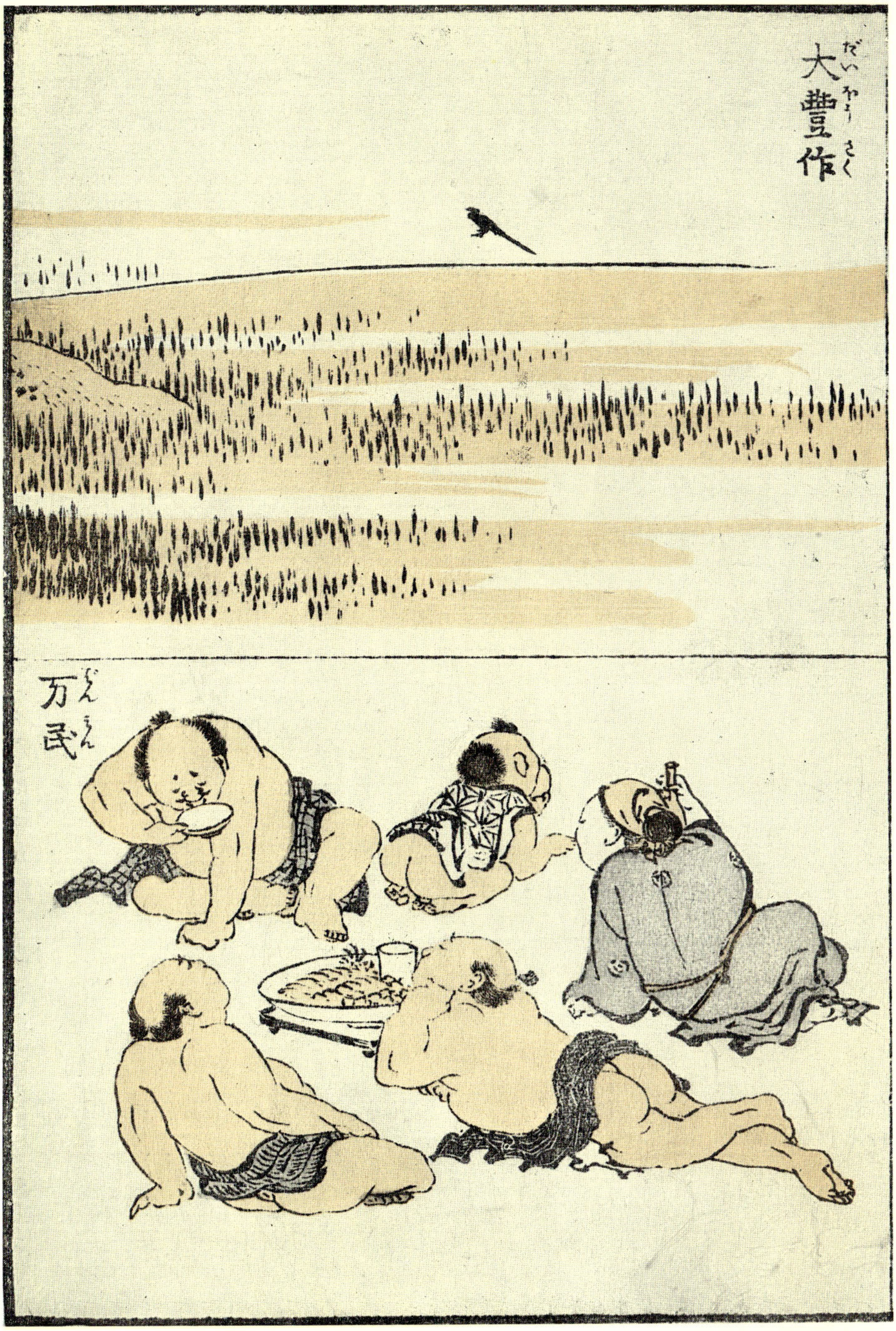

was liable to occur in rapid succession. Yet even in the most disastrous year, tithes still had to be paid to the local lord. It was only after an especially good harvest that the peasants could eat and drink their fill.

29. *Thin Types.* A skinny body may make for an elegantly willowy appearance when covered with a kimono (top center), but it scarcely engenders the same amused affection as a set of plumply rounded curves. The man preparing fish in the lower left-hand corner would almost certainly have been bad for trade; in *sushi* restaurants, for example, it was almost a requirement for success that the assistants should be young, fair-skinned, and well-fleshed.

30. *The Bathhouse.* Nowadays, the public bathhouses—with the exception of turkish baths, which are quite a different affair, at any rate—are gradually waning in popularity. In the Edo period, however, when few homes had their own bathroom, the bathhouses flourished, and it was one of life's greatest pleasures to meet friends and acquaintances there in the evening after a hard day's work. The woman with the band around her waist is pregnant. The woman with the shaven head busily shaving her cheek (it is quite common for women to shave in Japan, though scarcely necessary) is obviously a nun. Notice the skillful treatment of the naked body, a relatively uncommon theme in Japanese art.

31-32. *Watery Amusements.* Swimming as a sport seems to have a long history in Japan, since it is mentioned in Heian period documents. The emphasis, however, seems to have been less on speed, as today, than on various other skills. For example, during the Edo period the trick of "riding" a horse across a river (left-hand page, bottom) was regularly demonstrated every June in the Sumida River in Edo, and the shogun himself was often among the spectators. All the figures here capture the special buoyancy acquired by a body in water. Notice the figures with "lifebelts" at the upper right, and the eccentric figure at the top of the left-hand page who peers out at the watery activity from within a huge glass jar.

浮腹巻

33-34. *Sparrow Dance.* A popular humorous dance suggested doubtless by the pert, lively movements of sparrows. On these two pages Hokusai achieves an extraordinary variety of postures and a striking sense of movement—an effect that is enhanced when the figures are viewed as intended, in vertical rows from top right to bottom left. It is as though the artist was aiming at an illusion of actual movement, just as a child draws pictures on the corners of the pages of a book, then flicks them through to achieve a similar effect.

35-36. *Sumo Wrestling.* A large *dohyō* (the "ring" of sumo) is shown bottom center, with two pairs of wrestlers on it. The remainder of the two pages is occupied with examples of some of the principal holds, throws, and thrusts. In the Edo period, the sumo wrestler was considered to be the embodiment of masculine beauty, and he enjoyed enormous popularity. At that time, the tournaments in Edo were in fact limited to ten days each year,

in the grounds of the Ekōin temple in the Ryōgoku district (still the home of sumo). The two figures with a *gyōji* (referee) between them on the left-hand page are limbering up before a bout.

37-38. *Martial Arts.* On the left-hand page are shown two *ninja* at their business. The *ninja* was a type of paid agent who dealt in spying, assassination and the like, and whose skill depended on agility, invisibility, and various ingenious equipment. Their persons and the tools of their trade have acquired a kind of glamor in the mind of the general public that gives them a perennial popularity in period films and boys' magazines. The right-hand page shows, above, a judo throw, and below, a throw using *karate,* a technique of weaponless combat originally developed in the Ryukyus.

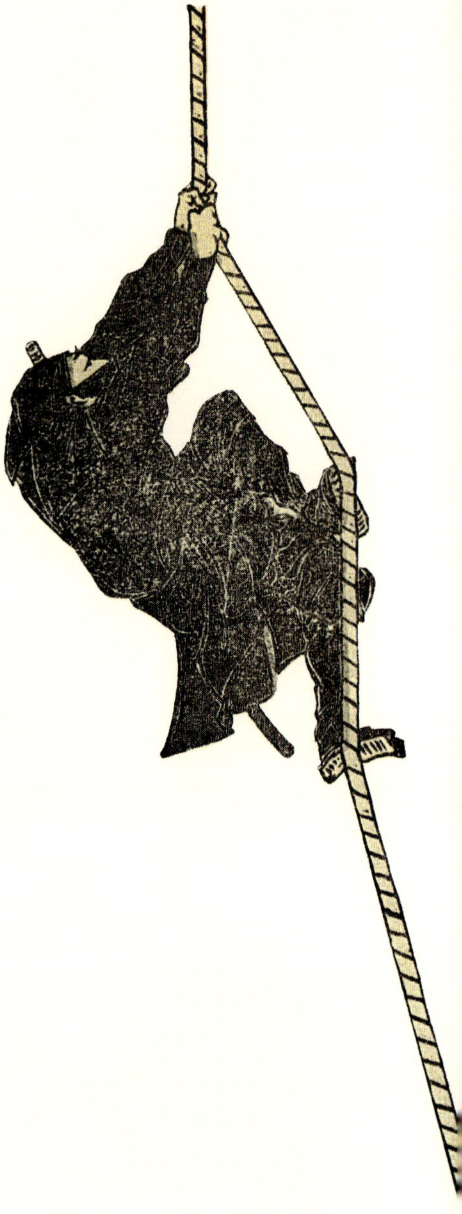

39-40. *Kendō. Kendō* refers to the art of Japanese fencing practiced mainly as a type of spiritual discipline. Normally the participants, as seen in the left of these two pictures, wear protective masks, breastplates, and armlets, and the swords are made of wood or bamboo. The highest development of the art of fencing came in the Edo period, when the samurai was seldom called upon to use his sword in actual battle—though the continued practice of wearing two swords whenever he went out offered a constant temptation to the more hotblooded of his class.

41-42. *Autumn Harvest.* This type of picture can be traced back to early times in China, where sets of scenes showing agricultural life throughout the four seasons—the preparation of the paddy fields, the sowing of the seed, the irrigation work, the ripe grain, the harvest—were popular subjects for folding screens and sliding doors. The idea was also taken over in Japanese art, but the ukiyo-e, though an art of the common people, generally concerned itself little with such themes. Hokusai, who was fond of referring to himself as a "peasant," was the great exception. On these two pages, beginning at the upper right, the various stages of harvest-

ing are shown, from reaping to threshing to the filling of the straw sacks used for transporting the grain, with a typical display of virtuosity in the figures of the men lifting and carrying the bales. Hokusai seems especially interested in the relationship between posture and center of gravity.

43–44. *In the Rats' Lair.* Anthropomorphized foxes, badgers, and cats are popular subjects in Japanese art and literature, and rats occasionally make their appearance even in the kabuki drama. Hokusai had already done the illustrations for a popular book of tales entitled *Legends of Supernatural Rats,* and it was inevitable that this type of subject should turn up somewhere in the *Sketchbooks.* The rats, who have stolen rice and other grain from human habitations, have brought their loot back to their own secret lair and are baling it

and complimenting themselves on a good harvest. There are even rats engaged in marking down tributes of rice in a big ledger, and another rat busily at work with an abacus. The picture is reminiscent of the famous Heian period picture scroll *Chōjū Giga*.

45-46. *Horses.* Two contrasted pages, the left-hand page containing five studies of horses done in considerable realistic detail, the right-hand page a single, stylized study of a wild horse done with a minimum number of brushstrokes. The latter type is generic to the Chinese style of painting; a similar horse occurs in a work attributed to the celebrated painter Sesshū.

47-48. *Running Tiger*. In China, the king of the beasts was the tiger. The lion was not indigenous to the country, and almost the only knowledge of lions came from sources such as the formalized beasts of Indian Buddhist painting. The unrealistic lion of Chinese art turned up again, at a still greater remove from reality, in Japanese art, where it was known as *karajishi* ("Chinese lion"). The tiger, on the other hand, was treated comparatively realistically. It was often shown in painting along with the dragon, which was supposed to rule the heavens just

as the tiger ruled the earth, or on sliding doors and screens as the "tiger in the bamboo grove." A real tiger had been brought to Japan by the Portuguese around 1600, but whether or not Hokusai had ever seen one is not clear; either way, the treatment here is close to nature.

49–50. *The Gods of Thunder and Wind.* In the East, powerful natural phenomena such as earth, fire, water, and so on have often been worshiped as gods and depicted in various grotesque forms. The gods of Thunder and Wind are two typical examples. In esoteric Buddhist portrayals they are dignified as gods clad in helmets and armor, but in popular lore the Thunder God is a demon who carries a large ring made of linked drums that he beats with sticks held in both hands. The Wind God, on the other hand, rushes about

the heavens carrying a large bag containing the winds on his back. Japanese paintings exist showing the two gods together in one picture—in medieval Buddhist art, for example—but the most famous work they inspired was the celebrated pair of screens by Sōtatsu.

51. *Monsters.* An enlargement of one section of a page devoted exclusively to such grotesque creatures. In later life, Hokusai began to be interested less in actual life and society than in the theoretical, the imaginary, and the historical or legendary. One outcome was the kind of alarming fantasy shown here. The public taste for this type of work can probably be attributed in part to the spiritual decadence and unease that marked the closing years of the Tokugawa Shogunate.

52. *Two Demons.* Another of Hokusai's grotesqueries. A demon is doing his shopping. He holds a large bottle of saké and a basket containing a large fish and a human head—destined, presumably, to be enjoyed along with the drink. Another demon holds out the account book in which details of the first demon's shopping are entered.

53-54. *The Vengeful Spirit of Kasane and the Priest Yūten; the Ghost of Okiku and Saint Mikazuki.* According to legend, Kasane was an ugly woman who was killed by her husband on account of her excessive jealousy. She came back to earth as a ghost and took her revenge, but eventually attained spiritual release through the intercession of the priest Yūten. The story was well known, and appeared in both literature and drama. Okiku was a maid who broke a precious

dish belonging to her master, who killed her in a fit of rage. He threw her body down a well, but her ghost appeared to exact its vengeance. Saint Mikazuki, almost certainly, was the priest whose incantations finally released her soul.

55. *Yamauba.* Yamauba (the "Mountain Hag," though in many of her appearances she is neither old nor hideous) appears in two principal forms in literature and legend. In one form, known chiefly from a celebrated Nō play, she is a strange woman living in the mountains who is encountered by a courtesan on her way from the capital to worship at the Zenkōji temple in Shinano Province. In her other form she is the mother of Sakata Kintoki (Kintarō), a boy of ruddy complexion and prodigious strength who represents a kind of ideal of the sturdy, pampered male child. In this second form she was often portrayed along with Kintoki by ukiyo-e artists, notably Utamaro and Kiyonaga, but in this picture Hokusai seems to be showing the less popular Yamauba of the Nō play tradition.

56. *Sayama Lake in Musashi Province.* Sayama Lake—on Sayama Hill, on what is now the border between metropolitan Tokyo and Saitama Prefecture—now serves as a reservoir for the capital. In Hokusai's day the lake was well known for its turtles, which on summer nights were sold at stalls along with goldfish and the like.

57-58. *The Princess Ta of Yin and Sun Wu-k'ung.* The Princess Ta was captured by Chow-wang of Yin when he defeated Yu Su-shih. She became his favorite, a woman noted for her licentiousness and cruelty. She was later slain by Wu-wang. Tradition has set her up as the archetype of the evil woman. Sun Wu-k'ung is the "hero" of the fantastic Chinese tale known in English as *Monkey*. A monkey endowed with magical powers, he causes wide-

spread consternation until he is finally subdued by the power of Buddhism. He subsequently accompanies the priest Hsüan-tsang to India, where he helps him acquire copies of the 5,048 scrolls containing the Buddhist canon.

59-60. *The Uncanny Strength of the Widow Oiko.* A warrior much proud of his own strength is on his way to participate in a wrestling contest in Kyoto, when a woman walking along a country path catches his fancy. He stretches out a hand to grasp her arm, only to find it caught in a viselike grip, and he is dragged along to her home (she is a widow), where she keeps him for three weeks, feeding him food and saké to make him "really strong." From around the age of fifty, Hokusai ceased drawing slender, doll-like women and switched to the older, more substantial type of femininity shown here.

61–62. *Fuki at Akita in Dewa Province. Fuki* is a plant resembling rhubarb. Its stalk proper is very short and is concealed in the earth, but it has petioles some 30–70 cm. long, surmounted by large leaves. The petioles, together with the portion extending beyond the leaves that bears the flowers, are edible. Particularly large *fuki* are found in the colder areas of Japan, especially Akita Prefecture. This picture shows an amusing exaggeration, with its *fuki* leaves stretching well over the heads of the three farmers, one of whom is using a leaf in place of a raincoat.

63–64. *Shallow Waters.* Since many of Japan's mountains are steep and lie close to the sea, rivers tend to be rapid, but in the dry autumn and winter seasons the flow becomes smaller and the rivers narrower and shallower. Here, three men—an itinerant monk, a traveler, and a woodcutter—are seen traversing the bed of such a river. The work is a simple one, done in a small picture book with two shades of black ink and one of light brown, yet it is extremely impressive, especially the treatment of the flowing lines that represent the water. It also succeeds wonderfully in suggesting the desolation of autumn and the long, lonely journey that lies ahead of the wayfarers.

65–66. *Plovers Over the Creek*. It is spring, for the old willow tree, bent so low over the water that its main trunk has disappeared beneath the surface, is putting out new buds on its remaining boughs. There is evidently a strong breeze over the water, which is broken by irregular ripples. Plovers fly past in groups, crying as they go. The work is simple, yet it is full of atmosphere, and the composition is excellent.

67–68. *Snow-Covered Bay in the Country*. In the *Sketchbooks*, Hokusai had to rely on two shades of black and one of light brown for all his effects, so that his achievement in this work resembles the Chinese-influenced ink painting with light color popular in the Muromachi period. In the same way, his "Hundred Views of Mount Fuji," with their varying shades of black, recall the *hakubyō* of the Heian period. The technical skill of this picture will be clear if one considers that Hokusai worked with three separate blocks, leaving large areas of the paper uncolored to represent the snow.

69-70. *Mount Fuji in Early Summer.* Snow still lingers near the summit. Since the left of the picture, where there is more snow, must be the north, the pine-covered shore in the foreground probably represents Miho-no-Matsubara, a famous beauty spot. Hokusai makes skillful use of the unprinted white paper to suggest snow and clouds, and of masses of broken black for the lower mountains, reserving his clean lines for the peak of Mount Fuji. It is a picture worthy of the man who was later to produce the celebrated "Red Fuji" of the "Thirty-six Views."

71–72. *Naruto Whirlpools in Awa Province.* Hokusai traveled west from Edo, gathering material for his work, on at least two occasions. He seems to have visited Nagoya, Nara, Osaka, and Kyoto, but it is not clear whether he went farther still and saw the famous Naruto whirlpools, which are caused by a difference in tide levels on either side of the straits between Awaji Island and Shikoku. Either way, the aim here is not to depict a specific place so much as to study water in violent, swirling motion. For Hokusai, movement in any form was a source of fascination, and moving water figures on several other pages of the *Sketchbooks.*

阿波の
鳴戸

73–74. *Whirlpool.* Here, Hokusai takes one of the whirlpools of the preceding picture and subjects it to closer scrutiny. A focus is given to the picture by the promontory that juts out over the sea, seeming to cleave the waters that swirl towards and away from the shore. The sense of pulsating movement towards the center of the whirlpool and the feeling of large masses of water are well conveyed.

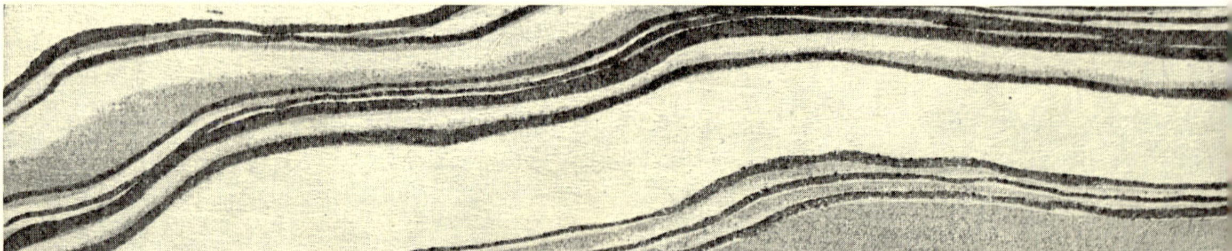

渦巻水

75. *Woman Holding a Cat in Her Arms* ◆ 9.1×7.9 inches (23.0×20.0 cm.) ◆ The remaining works reproduced here are not from the "Sketchbooks," but a selection of sketches made from works now in the Freer Gallery. In this picture, a woman is clasping a pet cat to her bosom; it has leapt into her arms in fright, and she is staring at whatever has alarmed it. In the outlines of the clothing Hokusai makes skillful use of all available types of brushstroke to suggest the movement that has just ceased.

76. *Woman Tuning a Samisen* ◆ 9.8 × 8.3 inches (24.8 × 21.0 cm.) ◆ The three strings of the samisen, a plucked instrument, are loosened when it is not in use. The woman here has tightened them and is now adjusting the pitch for playing. Concentration is skillfully suggested: her eyes are lowered, intent on her fingers as they work, and a slight frown knits her eyebrows. Hokusai was particularly clever at catching his subjects in such unguarded moments, and no mood, however fleeting, eluded the skill of his brush.

77. *Woman Doing the Cleaning* ◆ 12.4×9.0 inches (31.4×22.9 cm.) ◆ Carefully, so as not to disarrange her combs and hairpins, a woman binds a towel round her hair to protect it from the dust, while a broom that she has leaned against her body starts to fall to the floor. Once again one is impressed at Hokusai's genius for capturing the fleeting moment.

78. *Two Women Walking* ◆ 12.9×9.4 inches (32.7×23.9 cm.) ◆ The woman on the left is apparently just going out, for she wears high wooden clogs and is carefully adjusting the neck of her kimono as she goes. The woman on the right, who is barefooted, is presumably indoors. She has removed one of the wooden pins from her hair and is scratching her scalp with it as she goes, a common sight in the days of the traditional hairstyles, which were cumbersome and thickly plastered with oil.

79. *Courtesan Walking Along the Street* ◆ 15.2×8.9 inches (38.5×22.5 cm.) ◆ The posture, with the shoulders back and the abdomen thrust forward, is traditional to Japanese art, and can be seen in works as early as the Buddhist figures of the Asuka period. The design on the outer garment repays close attention, for the sense of motion in the waves of the sea, and of life in the plovers that breast the sea-breeze is worthy of Hokusai at his best.

RONIN GALLERY
605 Madison Avenue
New York, N. Y. 10022